This journal belongs to

_____

"I SAY, FOLLOW YOUR BLISS AND DON'T BE AFRAID,
AND DOORS WILL OPEN WHERE YOU DIDN'T KNOW
THEY WERE GOING TO BE."

—JOSEPH CAMPBELL

MAKE LOVE NOT WAR

LOVERS
DREAMERS
&ARTISTS

FREE SPIRIT

PEACE

"[IN THE 1960s] WE WERE YOUNG, WE WERE RECKLESS,
ARROGANT, SILLY, HEADSTRONG ... AND WE WERE RIGHT!
I REGRET NOTHING!"

—ABBIE HOFFMAN

MAKE LOVE NOT WAR

LOVERS
DREAMERS
&ARTISTS

FREE SPIRIT

PEACE

"THINK FOR YOURSELF AND QUESTION AUTHORITY."

—TIMOTHY LEARY

MAKE LOVE NOT WAR

LOVERS
DREAMERS
&ARTISTS.

FREE SPIRIT

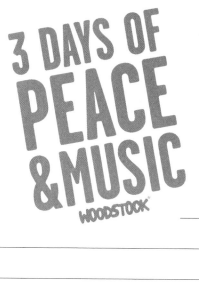

PEACE

"PEACE CAN BE MADE ONLY BY THOSE WHO ARE PEACEFUL,
AND LOVE CAN BE SHOWN ONLY BY THOSE WHO LOVE."

—ALAN WATTS

MAKE LOVE NOT WAR

LOVERS
DREAMERS
&ARTISTS

FREE SPIRIT

"LIKE WOW, THESE PEOPLE ARE REALLY BEAUTIFUL,
THE COPS, THE STOREKEEPERS, THE ARMY, EVERYBODY."

—LAURA GLAZER, A WOODSTOCK ATTENDEE

MAKE LOVE NOT WAR

LOVERS
DREAMERS
&ARTISTS.

FREE SPIRIT

"DON'T BOTHER MAX'S COWS. LET THEM MOO IN PEACE."

—SIGN AT WOODSTOCK

MAKE LOVE NOT WAR

LOVERS
DREAMERS
&ARTISTS.

FREE SPIRIT

"GOOD MORNING! WHAT WE HAVE IN MIND IS
BREAKFAST IN BED FOR 400,000."

—WAVY GRAVY, SPEAKING FROM THE STAGE

MAKE LOVE NOT WAR

LOVERS
DREAMERS
&ARTISTS.

FREE SPIRIT

"THE WHOLE THING IS A GAS. I DIG IT ALL, THE MUD,
THE RAIN, THE MUSIC, THE HASSLES."

—SPEED, A WOODSTOCK ATTENDEE

MAKE LOVE NOT WAR

LOVERS
DREAMERS
&ARTISTS.

FREE SPIRIT

PEACE

"I'M NOT WORRIED ABOUT THE SECURITY PARTICULARLY. IF PEOPLE HAVE ENOUGH TO DO, THERE WON'T BE TROUBLE."

—WESLEY A. POMEROY, HEAD OF SECURITY AT WOODSTOCK

MAKE LOVE NOT WAR

LOVERS
DREAMERS
&ARTISTS.

FREE SPIRIT

3 DAYS OF PEACE & MUSIC

August 15, 16, and 17, 1969. Woodstock Music & Art Fair organizers expected 50,000 attendees. They'd had trouble securing a venue until dairy farmer Max Yasgur agreed to let them use his 600-acre farm in Bethel, New York. Until April, they'd also had trouble signing popular performers. But when the festival began, more than 400,000 attendees arrived. By the time it ended, 32 of the most iconic rock and folk acts of the 1960s had taken the stage. They played in the sun, the rain, and the middle of the night. Rock & roll legends were created, a generation was defined, and music was changed forever.

FRIDAY

5:07	Richie Havens
7:10	invocation from Swami Satchidananda
7:30	Sweetwater
8:20	Bert Sommer
9:20	Tim Hardin
10:00	Ravi Shankar
10:50	Melanie
11:55	Arlo Guthrie
12:55	Joan Baez

SATURDAY

12:15	Quill
1:00	Country Joe McDonald
2:00	Santana
3:30	John Sebastian
4:45	Keef Hartley Band
6:00	The Incredible String Band
7:30	Canned Heat
9:00	Mountain
10:30	Grateful Dead
12:30	Creedence Clearwater Revival
2:00	Janis Joplin with the Kozmic Blues Band
3:30	Sly and the Family Stone
5:00	The Who
8:00	Jefferson Airplane

SUNDAY

2:00	Joe Cocker and the Grease Band
6:30	Country Joe and the Fish
8:15	Ten Years After
10:00	The Band
12:00	Johnny Winter
1:30	Blood, Sweat & Tears
3:00	Crosby, Stills, Nash & Young
6:00	Paul Butterfield Blues Band
7:30	Sha Na Na
9:00	Jimi Hendrix/Gypsy Sun & Rainbows

ISBN 978-1-64178-021-6

Fox Chapel Publishing makes every effort to use environmentally friendly paper for printing.

We are always looking for talented authors. To submit an idea, please send a brief inquiry to acquisitions@foxchapelpublishing.com.

Printed in China
First printing